FEDERACION ESPAÑOLA DE CICLISMO

«TROFEO MOSCARDÓ»

Ferraz, 16 - MADRID - Tels. 242 84 21 - 242 84 34 - 242 83 41

1978

LICENCIA N.° NA-47

VALEDERA HASTA EL 31 DE DICIEMBRE

Apellidos ...... INDURAIN LARRAYA

Nombre ...... Miguel ....

Fecha nacimiento 16-7-64 ....

Residencia ...... VILLAVA ....

Domicilio ...... c/ San Andrés, 2

Profesión ...... E. ....

Grupo Sanguíneo (...........) rh (...........)

Sociedad E. C. I. C. C. VILLAVES

Colores ...Verde...y...Blanco.........

CATEGORIA:

CADETE

PERTENECE A LA FEDERACION

NAVARRA

Miguel
INDURAIN

Noël Truyers

End
of the reign

21st September 1996: the day of the most crucial stage of the Tour of Spain. The leaden sun melts the tarmac and dehydrates the riders. At the foot of the final climb, Laurent Jalabert and race leader Alex Zülle unleash their most important attack of the race. They are faced with a fourteen kilometre ascent to the summit of Covadonga. Fourteen kilometres of narrow road, where only an occasional pine tree dotted here and there provides some shade. Even the toughest riders, staring up at the summit, have to pull out all the stops to tackle the steep slopes of the climb.

The Vuelta is destined to live out one of its most decisive episodes. But Spain in general is not really all that bothered about the clash of the Titans that is taking place under her very eyes. It is more interested in another struggle, the fight Miguel Indurain is having with himself at the other end of the race. Miguel Indurain: the god, the hero, the five times winner of the Tour de France, double winner of the Giro, World and Olympic time-trial champion has just decided to abandon the Vuelta. His pride hurt, and with seriously low morale, Indurain has taken his foot off the pedal on the penultimate climb of the day, the Mirador de Fito pass: he knows he can no longer keep up with his rivals. Herminio Diaz Zabala, former winner of Tirreno-Adriatico, cannot believe his eyes when he finds himself alongside an Indurain who has gone completely adrift. The bald ONCE rider tries all he can do to encourage the

"El Rey": his last press conference.
(Photo: RUG)

prestigious rider to continue, but it is no good. After putting a friendly arm round his shoulder, he continues his ascent alone. *El Rey* continues climbing slowly on the right-hand side of the road. With a look of resignation he fumbles in the pocket of his jersey to extract the little route-map, and having given it the once-over he shakes his head. Come what may, the Spaniard continues using the big ring. But he is getting slower and slower.

Ahead, Jalabert and Zülle - the two team-mates - are locked in a combat of epic proportions. Jaja finally wins the stage and the Swiss rider reinforces his hold on the *maillot amarillo*. Meanwhile, Indurain has been swallowed up by the *bus*. You can sense everything from incomprehension to complete surprise amongst the looks on the faces of the group of slow-moving riders. For several minutes, Indurain remains on their wheels. He has just one more mountain to climb. But at the point where the group passes by the team hotel where Banesto will stay after the stage, Indurain abandons. *"I'm riding on empty, I've had enough"* murmurs the five-time winner of the *Grand Boucle* before he disappears into the hotel. The Navarran giant has pulled out of the only major Tour which is missing from his *palmares*. And at the same time, he has settled a score with his sponsor, because Indurain had not wanted to ride this Vuelta, claiming that he did not feel he was in good enough form to do so.

And thus the emperor abdicated. Indurain would continue riding in the end-of-season criteriums but after the one held in Xativa he was never to be seen wearing his team kit again. The curtain finally fell on a long reign. There can be no doubt at all that Indurain was not physically worn out. But in terms of his morale, he was completely used up. Winner of the Tour of Asturias, the Bicicleta Vasca and the Dauphiné some months before, *El Rey* had been deposed in July during the Tour. He had recovered some of his former power when he won the Olympic time-trial but this was his farewell to arms. In the Vuelta, his weaknesses had been exposed and a saturation with cycling in general delivered the *coup de grace*. Kelme, Polti and ONCE began to push for Indurain's services for 1997, but Miguel had had enough. Unless one of them was kind enough to provide him with a salary of 30 million pounds, that is, an amount which would have made him change his mind, but which ONCE finally decided not to invest in the five-time winner of the Tour de France. "That's their problem" would seem to sum up nicely Indurain's attitude, who retired to his

villa in Olatz for the New Year celebrations. And he organised a press conference in a hotel for January 2 to break the news to the world: "I have devoted a great part of my life to the bicycle. For the past few weeks I have been weighing up the pros and cons of hanging up the bike. And I have finally decided that for the good of my wife and my family, it's best to stop. This decision has nothing to do with a feeling that I was physically incapable of winning a sixth Tour de France. Frankly, I think I could win a sixth Tour. But I'm stopping. I'm 32 and I want to spend my time doing other things."

Thousands of his fans were waiting at the doors of the hotel to give him a final send off: at the same time it was a clear sign of their approval of the Navarran's decision. Eddy Merckx gave Indurain's decision the thumbs-

Miguel will never have painful legs again.
(Photo: RUG)

up as well; indeed, he had not expected the Spaniard to take so long to reach it: "When super-stars like Indurain start haggling over the conditions of a contract, it's clear that the end is nigh. A rider who is motivated makes concessions much more easily. He has got other priorities: the team, the men he would like to have supporting him. Miguel no longer had these priorities."

Down on the **farm** in Villava

Miguel Indurain has changed the course of cycling history. It would have been completely different had the Spaniard not moved away from the career he seemed to be destined for: farming. After all, his parents were smallholders and ever since he had been a child Miguel had always loved tractors. And initially his love of the land was far greater than his devotion to cycling and to cycling's idols, of whom he knew the bare essentials, nothing more. Miguel had heard of Merckx and Anquetil, he was a serious fan of Bernard Hinault, but in no way was he inspired by these riders to go on to do great things of his own. Villava is a small village of 6,500 inhabitants in the foothills of the Pyrenees and is effectively not much more than a dormitory town for Pamplona, the capital of Navarre. Life passes there like a long slow river. If Indurain had not become the champion that we all know and love you can rest assured that we would never have heard of Villava, its bus stop, its two churches and the paper factory which employs half the local working population.

Chickens

Miguel Indurain Larraya was the oldest son of Miguel senior and Isabel Larraya, owners of their farm - which has a small acreage. They have a few vines for their own wine and also brew their own beer. Up at the crack of dawn, Miguel's parents go to bed when the sun sets on Navarre. Their farm is at the end of a cul-de-sac, three hundred metres away from a heavily used A-road. The noise from the traffic is a constant distant murmur in the background, partially blocked out by the hangars that stand between, and dulled by the cackles of the

A lover of the great outdoors.
(Photo: Jan Van der Perre)

Miguel, the yellow jersey and his parents.
(Photo: RUG)

poultry and the gusting wind - that brings, in turn, a strange smell of paper from the near-by factory.

30 hectares

The Indurains are the last survivors of a dying breed. Prudencio, the youngest son, is perhaps the only one who will continue on the farm - after he stops racing as a pro. But not Miguel. "I had thought for a long time that Miguel would follow in my footsteps" comments Miguel senior. "We have five children: Miguel, Isabel, Maria Dolores, Maria Asuncion and Prudencio. Miguel was the only one who seemed interested in working on a farm. It's a tough job, farming. We have 30 hectares of land to keep us busy. I was helped out by one of my brothers and his son. But the paper factory got bigger and bigger and they started building housing estates all round the village - which meant that we couldn't expand: we've had to make the most of what we've got and work hard in the process. We were always outdoors and Miguel liked that."

Stolen

And so it was that the Indurains' oldest son did not follow the path that seemed to have been laid down for him, but opted instead for a career on a bike. "And that happened by pure chance", remembers Miguel senior, "when he was ten years old, he had a little bike even though what he really liked doing was driving a tractor. He couldn't keep still for a minute. Personally, I never thought he

5

would really end up being a cyclist. Until one day after school he came to the fields to give me a hand. I was having a bite to eat and, just like always, he was enjoying himself driving the tractor. Suddenly he jumped down onto the ground. And he was livid. He had left his bike against a tree, but it had disappeared. But not before he had seen the thieves leaving at top speed. I jumped on the tractor and we tried to catch up with the two blokes but we never got Miguel's bike back. For a kid of eleven something like that is a complete disaster. So the next day we went into town to buy him another one. But this time we bought him a racer. He would have slept with it if we had let him...but at that time there was no question of him becoming a professional bike rider. Miguel was interested in working on the farm before doing anything else, especially as that involved lots of tractor driving..."

Athletics

Miguel has his own special memories of that time. He was not yet adolescent, but he was bursting with energy. "I liked riding bikes but I

The young Indurain in the company of Pepe Barusso, his very first trainer.
(Photo: Club Ciclista Villavés)

had lots of other interests. Like football, for example. And seeing as I was so big, they advised me to play basketball. Which I duly did but my long legs kept on getting tied up in knots. And in any case I wasn't really that interested in group sports. I far preferred sports where you acted alone, where I could decide what meant success and what meant failure for me. So when I was younger I started with a bit of athletics. I was even Navarran champion at 400 metres. But I gradually got more and more interested in riding a bike. Back home there was a bike club, the "Club Ciclista Villavés" and I joined it: even so, I still kept up the other sports and things stayed like that until I was 16."

32 wins at the age of 12.
(Photo: Club Ciclista Villavés)

6

The gifted rider

The club still exists. And every winter Miguel is the guest of honour at the club dinner. He makes it a personal obligation to attend, so he can present the cups and other awards to the most successful members of the club. When Miguel joined, the club had just 12 members. Now around 100 riders form part of it, trained and supported by five professional coaches, who have five cars to transport material and riders. The club accepts children from eight to 18. When they reach the upper age limit they move on to the club *Villavés Alas*, where Pepe Barusso, president and co-founder takes them under his wing. A man with a bike engraved on his heart. "From the first day I knew Miguel had something special about him"

Dynamite in his legs.

(Photo: Club Ciclista Villavés)

remembers the dark-haired Spaniard, proud to have put the champion on the right road to success.

32 victories

The young Indurain was big and well-built, with long black hair which spilled out from under his helmet when he was racing. And suddenly it became very apparent that Miguel had dynamite in his legs. "In his first race he came second. He was so proud of doing this that when he crossed the line he lifted up his arms as if he had won the race" remembers Barusso. "The following week, he got his first winner's bouquet, in his second race. Of course at that time there wasn't that strong a peloton and Miguel was clearly superior...he was gifted with a special way of riding the bike. He didn't muck around either, he would always give it all he had. When he was 12 he won 32 races just like that. But actually it made sense: whereas other young adolescents would be off trying out all kinds of things, Miguel already lived 100 per cent for the bike. He didn't smoke, he didn't drink, he never went out. He would divide his time between training, working on the farm and school. And he wasn't that interested in books either. He had been sent to a technical college where he learnt to make moulds. But when he turned 16 he quit. He wasn't that bad at science, but he hated other subjects - especially history."

How to identify Miguel Indurain (2nd from the right): neverending legs and built like an ox.
(Photo: Club Ciclista Villavés)

The **well-balanced** rider

The young Indurain had no kind of hang-ups. He took life as it came, enjoying his favourite activities and savouring his first sporting success. Almost on the sly, some scouts had already noticed that he had everything you need to be successful on the bike: incredibly long legs, a constitution like an ox, powerful lungs and a strong heart. He was perfectly well-balanced morphologically and physiologically, and this was going to help enormously to turn him into the champion of the future. Not to mention his qualities as a person - qualities which never failed to impress José-Miguel Echavarri, once his *directeur sportif*, first at Reynolds and then at Banesto.

A calm, confident individual, completely in control of his world.

The president

Echavarri and Indurain both live near Villava: about five kilometres separate their two houses. José Miguel was a professional himself, a *domestique* for Luis Ocana and Jacques Anquetil. But in the peloton of that time he never really acheived any kinds of results of note. And after hanging up the bike he became a hotelier along with his wife and became the owner of a beautiful 20-room property. But his passion for cycling suddenly returned and Echavarri knew he would have to return to it: "I never really changed professions... the evening they paid me a visit to ask me to direct the Reynolds amateur team, I barely hesitated before accepting."

From that time onwards, Echavarri acted as a filter for the innumerable requests from little clubs who wanted their best riders to join the prestigious team. And one fine day, Pepe Barusso, president of Villava CC, came knocking on his office door. "Pepe had a problem" remembers José Miguel and smiling as he does so. "In his club there was a young rider who simply oozed talent. So talented, in fact, that he had nothing left to learn in Villava. Barusso asked me to take him. "He's a good lad, a smallholder's son. You make sure you don't burn him out though" added Barusso. I listened hard to what Pepe had to say. I had already received a number of reports about this lad, but another six months passed before he was finally accepted into my team...".

The human diamond

Once in, however, Echavarri rapidly admitted what Barusso had told him was true: it was clear he just laid hands on a thoroughbred for his team. "After five minutes I understood absolutely everything" he laughed: and from then on his placid nature, whatever the circumstances, always had a beneficial effect on Indurain. "Ever since we first met, I have always been able to appreciate Miguel's natural strength. He was always incredibly serene, but that didn't mean he missed out on anything that was explained to him. He knew how to listen and how to apply the advice which was given to him. He wanted to learn and improve as fast as possible, but he was able to accept ideas that went somewhat against the face of convention. He had the gift of knowing how to sort out what was worthwhile and what was less so, and never rejecting out of hand anything that might be of the slightest advantage to him. And so right away I was able to appreciate I had hit upon a human diamond. And the results confirmed this impression. Effectively Miguel only spent two

From the very first day, his talent never stopped growing. (Photo: Club Ciclista Villavés)

years as an amateur. In his first season he won the Spanish national championships. The following year he took two stages of the Tour de L'Avenir. And he was just 20 when we suggested to him that he turned professional. Some months later he wore the *maillot amarillo* (the leader's jersey in the Vuelta) for five days. He was the youngest rider ever to have done so. We knew that all too well..."

The rouleur

If there was no doubting that Indurain was a 24-carat diamond, nevertheless some areas of the surface were in need of polishing and some corners needed filing down. This was a task which his entourage started to carry out on him at a very young age. "It might seem incredible" comments Pepe Barusso "but when he first began racing Indurain was a rouleur *par excellence*. As soon as they started putting the hammer down in the hills, Indurain would be out the back. He was well aware of this weakness. On other types of terrain, on the other hand, he was brilliant. And when he started he was a superb sprinter. And because of this, he had a disturbing tendency to put on

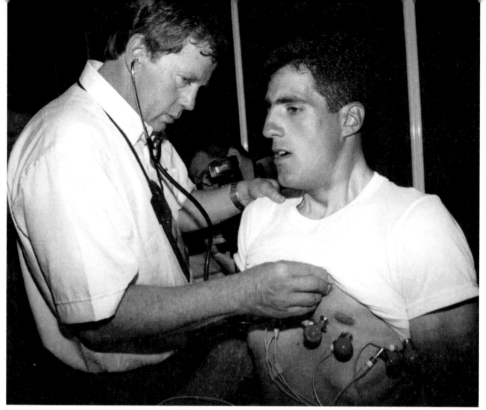

Resting heart rate: 28 beats per minute. (Photo: Luc Daelemans)

weight. I thought he was too well fed at home. Too much rich food on the kitchen table, which is exactly what all good farmers' boys get. We advised him to climb in his own style, avoiding any kind of drastic change of rhythm and to use his own tempo. From that day onwards, he never stopped progressing in the mountains."

Five kilos

At that time, Miguel Indurain rapidly worked out what it was going to take for him to improve at the demanding and highly specialised art of climbing on a bike. "Effectively, it was Doctor Conconi who really put me on the right road as regards climbing. He had worked with Francesco Moser for his attack on the Hour Record. Echavarri knew

him well, and he wanted us to go and pay him a visit. At the end of 1986, I had just won the Tour de L'Avenir. But on some mountain stages, I had felt too vulnerable and I was really worried about that. So we went to see Conconi. I did a whole series of tests, but what I really needed was his advice. I was fully developed as an adult by then and I was 1 m 88 tall and weighed 83 kilos: according to Conconi this was five kilos too much. So I went on a diet to lose those five kilos. And sure enough, from that moment onwards I felt much stronger in the mountains. Having said that there was no way I would ever become a super-climber like Pantani or Ugrumov. I was incapable of following specialists like them. Thank God, I always had the time-trials to fall back on and I could open up huge time-gaps there.".

The Perfect **Prototype**

Miguel Indurain was the prototype of the complete athlete, the personification of physical perfection. His incredibly long legs acted as top-quality pistons to produce power of devastating proportions. The other parts of his body helped create the perfect physiological context for him to exploit his potential one hundred percent. 1 metre 88 tall, in peak condition Indurain weighed in at 78 kilos. When he was racing he needed around 6,000 calories per Tour stage, which represented an average consumption of 1,200 calories per hour. The Spaniard's power output was enormous: thanks to his capacity to produce around 550 Watts he naturally became a master of the time-trial. There are a number of sprinters who are able to reach such a high level of power but they are only able to do so for a brief period of time. On the other hand, the Navarran champion was also endowed with an amazingly high lung capacity: nigh-on eight litres: thanks to this overdeveloped thoracic cage, he was able to breathe in 88 mililitres of oxygen per kilo per second.

Pulse

Another incredible piece of data about Indurain's physiological make-up was the following: his pulse rate was just 28 beats a minute when resting , which means less than one beat per two seconds. A good cyclotourist normally has a pulse rate of around 50 beats a minute. In the mountains, Miguel's pulse rate would frequently go over 150 but it would never go higher than 195. Tests have shown that in the space of one minute he could pump the equivalent of 50 litres of blood around his entire arterial system; that is double the blood pressure of a normal individual. Miguel would often analyse his body in the following way: "I didn't create my physical make-up. These qualities are innate. They are a gift from God."

A lung capacity of nearly 8 litres. (Photo: Luc Daelemans)

11

Knowledge

Furthermore, Indurain had developed a perfect level of self-understanding. At one with his body the Spaniard knew how to organise his preparation to reach peak condition at exactly the right moment. "It's something which is vital if you want to win the Tour. You have to be at 150 per cent for 23 days. It is never a good idea to waste a single ounce of energy before it is absolutely necessary. I've always been very attentive in that area. Trying as hard as I can not to overdo it in the time-trials. That was never too hard because I knew my body perfectly. There was never any need to look at my pulseometer to know if my muscles were producing lactic acid or not. It was an automatic sensation. When I felt it, I would ease up for the time I needed to. The rest was just a question of confidence and experience. Of course that didn't mean I couldn't be a victim of a puncture,

a technical problem or a crash. But I always tried to convince myself that that kind of thing wouldn't happen. And in fact I never suffered from too many doubts."

Stress

Indurain thus knew how to turn his exceptional physical attributes to his advantage and climb to the summit of the hierachy of cycling. At the same time, the Spaniard turned the pressure and stress that assailed him at the beginning of each Tour to his advantage. "In the evenings, no sooner had he closed his eyes than he would fall into a deep sleep" explained Echavarri. "And before he fell asleep, he would put the "maillot jaune" on the back of a chair as if it was just any old jersey from a race like the Tour of Vaucluse. That's the kind of thing that has never intimidated him. Whatever the reason he never missed out on a second of rest because of that jersey."
"That's definitely because of my

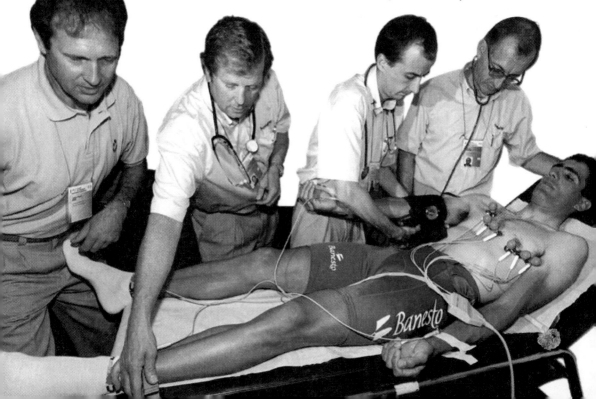

family", was Miguel's frequent explanation. "On the farm, my parents have always based their work around two elements: the weather and the harvest. Everything else was relative. If things went well, so much the better. If they didn't, so much the worse, there was nothing you could do. This was the philosophy in which I was educated and which I applied later to my racing." His *directeur sportif* has often praised Miguel's attitude to life: "He was a very calm, placid person, unfazed and unhassled by problems. But at the same time he was very ambitious and hard on himself. I've always been impressed by the amount of time he could spend alone in his room. He would avoid the slightest distraction to his well-being. Which is normal, in a sense, for a boy who grew up amongst the cackling of chickens and the sounds of the countryside. As a child, Miguel had ridden down quiet country lanes chewing on a piece of grass so often that he had built up a superb line of defence against anything the world could throw against him. The people of the land know that their life forms part of the weather, the sun, the rain, factors over which they have absolutely no control. They act using what nature gives them, without losing their heads. This was exactly Miguel's great strength. He never let himself be overwhelmed by the things that surrounded him."

Emotions

Furthermore, Miguel had the ability to control his emotions. In any circumstances, throughout his career, he was the epitome of courtesy and accessibility. Getting over-excited was something that never happened to him, as was being excessively disappointed when something went wrong. "During his career as a cyclist there

On the left: prodigious physical capacity.
(Photo: Luc Daelemans)

In the company of his inseparable "directeur sportif", José Miguel Echavarri.
(Photo: Philippe Lebeau)

were only three occasions when I saw him overwhelmed with happiness: once when he was recieved by the Pope, he was genuinely over the moon. It is true that he is a profound believer. And then in 1992 he was tremendously pleased when they chose him as sportsman of the year in Italy: he had just won his first Giro. In his country Miguel has also received the Prince of Asturias prize, the highest of distinctions. That day I felt he was really nervous: he had to appear on the podium with Liz Taylor and Nelson Mandela. But on other occasions it was necessary to impose certain conditions on him. I remember that when all the Olympic medallists were informed that King Juan Carlos wished to grant them an audience, Indurain decided not to bother with the invitation."

Patience

The Navarran star has always been notoriously capable of not rushing into things. Always willing to pay attention to good advice, Indurain was never one to burn himself out too quickly. In this context Pedro Delgado has played a decisive role for the rider who was destined to succeed him. In the shadow of Delgado, Miguel could expand gently and progressively. "Pedro was my reference point. I used to be able to lean on on his experience. But I never held him up as an idol. My cycling hero was always Bernard Hinault. I always admired Hinault's enormous sense of responsibility. Hinault was a real *patron*. Pedro was just an example for me to follow. He had the ability to live for a race, to give it everything he'd got, with a great deal of panache. Me, I was much less fiery. We've never really been good friends. We were too different from each other. Pedro was more active, freer. But I've always appreciated him a lot. He was the guy who had to take all the pressure, which gave me the chance to progress at my own speed and in a relaxed way. And that was indispensable: I was still very young. At 20, if you don't have enough time to progress, then its easy for everything to get shot to pieces in a moment."

Bearing the brunt

The greatest champion ever in Spanish cycling history waited patiently for his time to come. The general message to Miguel was "when events show that you are the best then they'll put you on the track." And Miguel's time arrived when he won his first Tour, in 1991. "Eusebio Unzue, whom I consider to be my first real trainer, had a vital role to play in my progression. He would never tire of telling me that I should never burn myself out too quickly. And he was right. When I was a young rider I was never that brilliant - at first. I rode as an amateur for two years. In 1983, my first year, I was Spanish national champion. But apart from that title, I had few other

successes. Then Unzue took me under his wing and the following season I won no less than 15 races. I rode in the Peace Race and the Los Angeles Olympics and I won two stages of the Tour de L'Avenir. After that Unzue decided that the time had come for me to turn professional. Perhaps it was a bit too early on. But by pure luck, there was Perico to bear the brunt."

Ocana

Not everybody believed that Indurain should be so protected and cosseted. Luis Ocana, former winner of the Tour, was firmly against the idea and had no hesitation in letting everybody know so. "Indurain spent too long in Delgado's shadow" was how the late lamented Luis put it. "He should have put Pedro under pressure far earlier. People have often criticised me for my over-aggressive character. And it was exactly that kind of obstinate, aggressive edge to his personality that Indurain was lacking." This kind of attack was like water off a duck's back for Miguel. "I have always dreamed of becoming a great rider. But I had absolutely no desire to set myself a time-table or place where this had to happen. I had the chance to learn my profession by Pedro Delgado's side. All the pressure and hassle was heaped on him. He had no right to make a mistake, while I could get along with doing my own thing."

On the right: the machine at top speed during a time-trial. *(Photo: Sergio Penazzo)*

Fame and glory have their pleasurable moments...
(Photo: Luc Daelemans)

Miguel Indurain worked like a teacher who knows his subject like the back of his hand. And just as a teacher adapts to the level of the class he has in front of him, the Spaniard changed his strategies depending on the rival he had to face. In other words he altered his approach according to the type of opposition present in the race. If they tried to attack him, Indurain attacked back, like the great strategist of psychological warfare he was as he grew older and wiser. Furthermore, given his capacity to read a situation Indurain always knew what his own limits were, trying never to go beyond them whatever happened. Basically, his tactic was devastatingly straightforward: he would open up huge gaps in the time-trials and then hold onto that advantage in the mountains before delivering the final blow in the second race against the clock. What was his favourite terrain for putting this three-fold plan into practice? the Tour de France. The "Grand Boucle", the race where five glorious chapters of his career were written, where he would join Eddy Merckx, Bernard Hinault and Jacques Anquetil at the very top of the cycling hierachy. With the only difference - and it is not an unimportant one - between the Spaniard and his illustrious predecessors: the Spaniard would ride onto the Tour de France as winner five times in a row. An unbroken reign. Miguel Indurain would finally end up taking part in eleven Tours. It was only the sixth time that his number finally came up. Before taking his first "maillot jaune", the Spaniard would follow a gentle upwards curve towards the summit: in 1986, he abandoned on the 12th stage, in 1987 he finished 97th, in 1988 he finished 47th, in 1989 he was 17th and won a stage and in 1990 he came tenth and took another stage win. And from that point onwards the road to glory in the Tour de France lay before him...

The general surrounded by his faithful soldiers. (Photo: Graham Watson)

1991 The fourth Spaniard

At the start of the Tour 1991, almost everybody put down Greg LeMond as the favourite to win. And in the first time-trial, LeMond managed to hang on to the yellow jersey, despite Indurain's impressive performance. But it was soon to become clear that the American was tired. He managed to give the impression that this was not the case as far as the foot of the Pyrenees, but no further. On the stage to

Val Louron Indurain showed his cards and formed an alliance with Claudio Chiappucci. The Spaniard took over the race leadership from Luc Leblanc, who had managed to gain the yellow jersey the evening before when the Tour reached Jaca. But it was really LeMond who collapsed: ironically, the American's great strength had always been a stubborn refusal to crack under the harshest of circumstances, and who had always declared that his favourite days on the Tour were the ones when the fight for the overall became a clear one. Admittedly Greg had shown great courage by attempting to attack on the Tourmalet, but this move proved to be the last one for the American. From that moment onwards, he went into an inexorable decline, scrabbling desperately at the bottom of the barrel to finally finish 7-18 down. Bugno, Fignon and LeMond had finished over three minutes down on the Navarran. In the '91 Tour, Miguel behaved as if he were a boxer, looking hard for the chance to deliver a knock-out punch. And on the penultimate stage he literally outclassed his most dangerous rivals in the final time-trial, Bugno losing 28 seconds in the process. Right up to the final stage on the Champs Elysées, it seemed as if Chiappucci was determined to knock Indurain off the throne which he had just inherited. But finally the Spaniard took his first victory in the Tour de France, 3-36 ahead of Bugno and 5-56 ahead of Chiappucci.

At 27, he became the fourth Spaniard, after Bahamontes, Ocana and Delgado, to write his name down in history as a winner of the Tour. "I have only one wish" confessed Spain's new hero as soon as he got off his bike for the last time in the Tour that year: "I just want to go home to Villava in a team car and enjoy a few quiet days there. Tomorrow I will have a day of complete rest, I won't do a thing. And then I suppose I will have to go and take part in a number of celebrations. But I won't overdo it."

The giant Spaniard's exploits had thrilled the world. Apart from Luis Ocana, who criticised Indurain again for not being overly aggessive: "Miguel has won, but in my opinion, he's not ambitious enough" was how the former Tour winner put it.

Bugno, Indurain and Chiappucci.
                    (Photo: Luc Daelemans)

1992 The extra-terrestrial

Miguel was highly motivated before the start of that year's Tour: the Spaniard had just won the Giro for the first time, and there was no way that he was going to miss out on his favourite race in San Sebastian, in front of his *public*, by not winning the prologue. Alex Zülle, Richard Virenque and Pascal Lino would follow the Spaniard in the yellow jersey. Not that it really mattered. Indurain was destined to wipe the floor with his rivals in the time-trial at Luxembourg. Chiappucci attempted to put some kind of excitement back into the Tour when he put in an epic ride to Sestrières. But Indurain intelligently kept everything under control, delivering his final blow in the final time-trial. Chiappucci, the best climber present, finished second at 4-35 and the worldchampion Gianni Bugno took third place on the podium, 10-49 behind Indurain. The 1992 race has gone down in history as being the fastest on record - for the moment. Not a day went by without some kind of attack putting the average speed for the race even higher and driving the time-keepers crazy. Even in this kind of situation Indurain showed his iron constitution once more. At the end of the day, just two moments briefly suggested possible weaknesses: "The first was on the stage to Brussels. It rained cats and dogs that day. Those are the kinds of weather conditions I loathe. I suffered really badly in Belgium. You couldn't see ten yards ahead. My only aim was to cross the finishing line in one piece." And the second moment of weakness came at Sestrières. Two kilometres from the summit Indurain blew spectacularly, allowing Chiappucci to open up a substantial gap by the finish. During this Tour, Miguel has no doubt that

Prudencio and Miguel Indurain: disturbingly similar. *(Photo: Sergio Penazzo)*

the most important moment of the race for him was the time-trial in Luxemburg. Turning the excellent road surface to his advantage, Indurain reached a state of perfection incarnate on the bicycle. Everything was in harmony: his pedalling style, his natural grace, the understanding between man and machine. Not even the slightest error tainted the Spaniard's race style, who accelerated steadily as the kilometres passed by. "He's a robot, a superman, an extra-terrestrial" spouted the sports dailies across the world, adding afterwards "at the art of riding alone on a bike, that is." Indurain was in such a state of grace that he gained between four and five seconds on his main rivals every kilometre. "At first, I thought I was going nuts" remembers his second *directeur sportif* Eusebio Unzue. "After the

When it came to time-trialling, Indurain was out of this world.   (Photo: RUG)

first 20 kilometres the average speed was 60 kilometres per hour! His bike had been equipped with a big ring of 56 and that enabled him to go at up to 70 kilometres per hour when he was riding full on. At the start there was a ten-minute time gap between the team car following Delgado and the one following Indurain. By the end of the route, Miguel had come so close to Pedro that we could hear the other directeur shouting encouragement at his rider without the slightest difficulty." Indurain annihilated his rivals' morale at Luxembourg. Without ever having to go above 190 beats per minute at any point during the time-trial, he had built up a vast protective barrier of time between himself and his enemies. And just a minute after he finished, Indurain's pulse had dropped again to 58. In a word, phenomenal.

Chiappucci, Indurain and Bugno.
*   (Photo: Luc Daelemans)*

1993 Not so **interesting**

Once again Indurain had finished the Giro wearing the pink leader's jersey. And from the prologue at Le Puy de Fou onwards, it was clear that Indurain was going to be the fastest of them all. Over the next few days, the yellow jersey moved from one pair of shoulder to another amongst the sprinter/*rouleur* tribe: Nelissen, Cipollini, Museeuw. But *El Rey* made a devastating move in the time-trial at Lac de Madine, and from that point on he reclaimed his property: only Tony Rominger seemed able, at that point, to be in some kind of position to challenge him. But

the Swiss rider seemed to be content merely with two stage wins in the Alps and the polka-dot jersey of King of the Mountains. Rominger finally finished second, 4-59 behind Indurain, while the surprising Polish rider Zenon Jaskula made it onto the podium for third place 5-58 down on the winner. Indurain barely had to exert himself to conquer his third Tour. The rivals seemed to be even weaker than in previous years, as Chiappucci started on a downwards curve and Old Father Time ensured Bugno began to lose his edge as well. Jaskula was finally the revelation of this *Grand Boucle*, but the Polish rider never showed himself to be capable of giving the Emperor of Pamplona any cause for concern. As for Rominger, a serious run of bad luck

*Rominger:
a courageous rival.*

undermined his morale way before his form was at its peak. And thus Indurain won his third Tour. The whole of Spain celebrated as one does in these circumstances, not without a slight sense of disappointment after what happened on the penultimate day's racing. In a time-trial that seemed to be made for him, Indurain was actually beaten by Rominger, who charged round the course at the speed of a TGV: Indurain on the other hand, seemed to be strangely uncomfortable. "I didn't want to take any risks" was his justification afterwards 'I eased up in the risky parts of the course. I simply thought I wanted to be sure I would take home the final victory. I only wanted to keep the yellow jersey. Tony on the other hand still had to bust a gut to ensure he would stay second overall. In those sorts of circumstances, there was a far greater chance that he would end up going faster..." There was not the slightest sign of delight to be found in the face of the Navarran rider, who celebrated his third win without any kind of triumphalist gesture. "The first week I concentrated on avoiding crashes. Even so I was caught in one mass pile-up, but fortunately there were no serious consequences. Just a little cut in the wrist. I opened up the main time difference at Lac de Madine: that day I was in a state of cycling grace. What remained afterwards was to get through the Alps and Pyrenees without suffering any kind of crisis. And things progressed as was expected, even when Rominger opened up a gap of 50 seconds on the Tourmalet, but I never panicked. My kind of physique was always a handicap on the big, steep climbs. But when I start to shift on the descents, on the other hand, that turns into a distinct advantage. Above all, I was pleased that I had no real bad days during three weeks' racing."

Rominger, Indurain and Jaskula.
(Photo: Luc Daelemans)

1994 The **easiest**

That year, Indurain was unable to take control of things in the Tour of Italy. Suddenly, many people started asking themselves what Indurain's real chances were of taking a fourth yellow jersey. But at Hautacam, the first big col on that year's menu, Indurain crushed all doubts and silenced his critics, who were increasingly critical of his overcautious approach and lack of panache. As if to answer them, Miguel put on an epic display of power, class and stamina. There can be no doubt that on the slopes of the Hautacam the Navarran giant wrote one of the most glorious pages of his career as a cyclist. In the first few kilometres of the climb it was Marco Pantani who opened fire

first, opening a gap of up to 40 seconds on the Navarran. It was at that moment that Miguel really opened up: using the same kind of force that normally he reserved exclusively for the time-trials. Standing on the pedals to use a massive gear, without ever looking back to see what happened behind him, Indurain set about dropping all those who wished to stay on his wheel and try as best they could to maintain contact. Zülle, Ugrumov, Tonkov, Virenque and the rest were all blown off the Spaniard's wheel, all of them asphyxiated, exhausted. And at the point where Indurain swooped like a bird of prey on Pantani, only Luc Leblanc remained with him at the head of the race. And in fact the Frenchman was able to win the stage. On the final podium, Indurain was flanked by Piotr Ugrumov (second at 5-39 and still in the grip of some understandable regrets about his performance) and by Pantani (third at 7-19 and with a glorious future stretching before him). The Spaniard had, once more, acheived his aim. He finished stronger than he had done in other years, bearing in mind that the opposition was even more limited. This fourth victory was perhaps the least impressive, but there was no denying Indurain had been an omnipresent force throughout the race. After Boardman's victory in the prologue, Museeuw, Vanzella, Yates and Museeuw for a second time had managed to lay their hands on the treasured yellow jersey. Indurain returned to his throne in the time-trial at Bergerac. After his royal performance in the Pyrenees, Indurain preferred to let others take the initiative in the Alps, where Pantani won one stage and Ugrumov won two. But the Spaniard stayed in control. "It doesn't matter how, what matters is to win the Tour" he commented in Paris. "I'm tired. But I don't doubt I'm less tired than a lot of other people. I haven't had one single difficult day. No collapses, no illness like I had last year. In 1993 I had to put up with Rominger's presence right the way through the Tour. This year I have shook off my rivals much more quickly. It's been a strange Tour: the riders everyone thought would be by my side have disappeared very quickly from the scene. I couldn't do anything about that and we all waited for things to come to a head in the Alps. But in fact everything was played out in the Pyrenees. It was there that I could strengthen my hold on the race after pulling ahead in the first time-trial. And looking at the race from that point of view you could say my team-mates have been brilliant. As a group they were very solid, very strong."

Miguel's birthday: a tradition in the Tour.
(Photo: Sergio Panazzo)

Ugrumov, Indurain and Pantani.
(Photo: Luc Daelemans)

1995 Peak condition

In the eyes of many, Miguel Indurain's 1995 Tour win was the most admirable of all, given that it was his fifth consecutive victory. Prior to the Spaniard nobody had succeeded in doing that: not even Merckx, Anquetil or Hinault. And above all this time, *The Master* had succeeded in doing so with a rare panache, dominating less strongly in the time-trials and instead laying an important part of the foundations for his triumph in the mountains. More than ever the Spanish machine seemed to be perfectly in order, without the slightest error being made from start to finish in the race.

Boardman fell badly in the prologue, allowing Durand to have the privilege of taking the first yellow jersey. The *maillot* then changed hands

to Jalabert, Gotti, Riis and Johan Bruyneel. But following the time-trial between Liège and Seraing, it moved once more onto Indurain's shoulders. The Spaniard would wear it from then onwards until the race finished in Paris, finally finishing 4-35 ahead of Alex Zülle and 6-47 up on Bjarne Riis.

Indurain sewed things up in two phases. During the stage which took the race to Liège, he found himself on the attack along with Bruyneel. Victim of the overall team strategy, Johan was unable to push Indurain hard. But in any case the Spaniard took complete control of his offensive in the Ardennes. The Belgian would win the stage at Liège when he outsprinted Indurain, taking the yellow jersey in the process. "My only objective was to put some time

And number five for El Rey...

between myself and climbers like Virenque and Pantani. This mission was successfully accomplished. Riis, Rominger and Berzin managed to limit the time gap, but I was far less worried about these three in the high mountain stages" was Indurain's analysis. Furthermore, the following day he was set to confirm his status as an exceptional *rouleur* on the stage between Huy and Seraing. However, Indurain decided to use a slightly smaller gear than the one used by most of his rivals - 54x12. But the effect was no less impressive than usual: Rominger lost 58 seconds during the time-trial, Berzin lost 38 and Riis just

12. "The end of the evening before, with Bruyneel on my wheel, had felt like a real time-trial. In that raid I lost a bit of my freshness. The course between Liège and Seraing was quite a tough one. I started very fast and I needed to ease up a bit at one point so I could finally finish full on." From that point on, Indurain was back in yellow and he was set to stay in yellow until the race reached Paris.

Alex Zülle decided to play his cards in the Alps on the stage to La Plagne. The Swiss rider even managed to become yellow jersey on the road before Indurain, more attentive than ever, put his house in order once more. Endowed with a considerable eagerness and physically on a high, Miguel had resolved not to race in a defensively, as had been his custom in previous years. This time the Spaniard, no longer riding the Giro, had kept his fuel tank intact and the result showed his strength.

"This time round it was less testing than the previous Tours" he claimed. "I had far fewer attacks to respond to, and some of my rivals had some kind of knee trouble. And lots of them were already exhausted even before the race started. That drop in concentration explains why there were so many crashes. The season really has got too long. Having said that, when your aim is to ride the Tour in order to win, you know you have to come to the start in peak condition."

27

Perfection in the lone effort.

The **Emperor's last waltz**

What was at stake in Indurain's eleventh Tour could not have been more straightforward. But his objective could not have been a more challenging one. A sixth win in the Tour de France would have made Indurain the first rider in history ever to achieve such an exploit. And what's more he would have gone down in the record books as having won the race on six consecutive occasions. At the start of the race, the general consensus was that Indurain would once more prove to be invincible, inaccessible. What actually happened was set to blow that attractive theory sky high. The Navarran giant had never once missed out on a date with destiny in the Tour in the previous five years. But he was doomed to lose his *punctuality* at Les Arcs, where his legs would suddenly refuse to work. In just a few kilometres, *El Rey* lost more than three minutes to Riis, Rominger, Berzin and Olano.

Hunger

After an event tinged with such peculiar intensity, the entire race was flung into a new dimension. The Emperor had just been dethroned. For the first time in his sporting career, devastated by the rain, hunger, and even dehydration, suddenly Indurain was on his knees, literally forced to drag himself

The old and the new: the power changes hands in Pamplona. *(Photo: AP)*

Riis pays homage to Indurain.

his grip on the *maillot* by winning the time-trial. Meanwhile, in the Banesto camp, there was a general agreement not to panic. "We are still feeling confident" was Echavarri's analysis "We've discovered the reason behind what happened the day before yesterday. Effectively it was because after removing and then putting on his rain-jacket again, Indurain sweated heavily - too heavily. This in turn caused a rapid drop in his calorie level, with the consequences that were there for all to see. If we had been able to give him something to drink immediately afterwards, then none of this would have happened. Fair enough, you can argue that the situation is new for us because we have never seen it before. But we are going to find the solution."

Sadly, over the following days, Indurain's physical condition simply worsened.

Explosion

When the sun returned Bjarne Riis rang Miguel's sporting death-knell on the slopes of Hautacam. The Spaniard lost 2-38 to the Dane, ironically enough on his birthday. "During the first few kilometres I used a 39x17. And then I saw Riis draw up close to me: he was riding on the big ring with un-nerving ease. I just couldn't believe my eyes. That was the knock-out punch for me. From that moment onwards I knew it would be practically impossible to undermine his hold on the jersey. Bjarne upped the pace four times, with incredibly brutal changes of speed. I could hold him three times, but on the fourth occasion, I simply blew up." sighed Indurain. The extra-terrestrial had suddenly fallen to earth, had been revealed as a mere mortal with all the defects and weaknesses that form a part of human nature. The following day, as the Tour headed towards Pamplona, Miguel was greeted with applause like he had never known before.

towards the summit, with a blank stare betraying the pain in his muscles. "I don't understand anything" stammered the fallen hero at the finish. "Six kilometres before the summit, I felt fantastic. I had even planned to attack on the final part of the climb when suddenly I cracked completely. Everything was blocked up. My legs felt incredibly heavy and weak. It was probably a case of a sudden lack of "fuel". I am sure that the rain brought that on, given that I've always had an extreme aversion to it. I've lost a battle today. But the Tour is not over yet."

No Panic

The following day, everybody was impatient for the Val D'Isere hilly time-trial to start. During the race against the clock Indurain gave the impression that he had partially recovered his strength. It was not enough, however, for him to make a challenge to Berzin's hold on the yellow jersey. The Russian had inherited it the evening before and reinforced

Three living legends of the Tour: Hinault, Merckx and Indurain.
(Photo: Jan Van der Perre)

Big Mig and
the Great Eddy

Come what may, from now on for many years to come Miguel Indurain will always be considered as a member of the elite club of five-time winners of the Tour de France. "Indurain was limited in the mountains. He lacked a capacity to suddenly explode. But against the watch it was another story: he was sublime, gifted with an incredible degree of stamina" sums up Eddy Merckx as he attempts to describe the character of the champion of Villava. "We are really going to miss his innate elegance on a bike. Having said that I find it hard to believe that he had come to the end of his natural strength. At the end of the day, he finished eleventh in that Tour, having already won the Tour of Asturias, the Bicicleta Vasca and the Dauphiné

Libéré in the same year. He had definitely peaked too early, at the wrong time of the season. Perhaps one solution would have been for him to delay hitting good form by putting on weight a little. But bearing in mind the appalling weather conditions in the first week of the Tour he risked not being able to use this extra weight in the mountains."

"That having been said, for someone who is not a thoroughbred climber, it's even harder to carry that excess weight. And on the other hand, there was no time-trial prior to the big days in the mountains, which meant that the climbers didn't really have to use all their reserves. No, from a technical point of view, it was impossible for Miguel to win this Tour" was the great Eddy's final conclusion.

One hour:
53.040 km

Such were his qualities as a *rouleur* that Miguel Indurain owed it to himself, at least once in his career, to try to break the World Hour Record. The Spaniard took a long time to decide to do so, because *El Rey* had other priorities. Finally it was on the 2nd September 1994 that he took to the track. At 2pm the Bordeaux velodrome had opened its doors to the public. Jose Miguel Echavarri had specifically requested that the sound engineers in the stadium put on *Chronology* by Jean-Michel Jarre, as the thousands of supporters who had come to support Miguel in his attempt poured onto the terraces. And the noise from the rattles hit fever pitch as Miguel appeared on his road bike to

His assault on the hour record happened in the logical kind of place. (Photo: Sergio Penazzo)

start his warm-up session. Thirty seconds later he changed his bike to almost immediately ride around the track in the wake of a derny motor. The session lasted around 18 minutes, apart from five minutes of recuperation time at a lower speed.

Silence

Echavarri then proceeded to guide his rider to the dressing cabins in the inner ring of the track, where Miguel received a final massage. At 2.54 pm the Spaniard adjusted his helmet and climbed back onto his saddle for a final warm-up: he started doing laps at around 19 seconds which gradually speeded up to laps of 17. This was the time he would have to maintain for an hour if he wanted to beat the Hour Record. 3.04 pm: the moment of truth had finally arrived. A silence that you could cut with a knife fell on the Bordeaux velodrome while Indurain concluded his last-minute preparations. And then the countdown started. One hour later, Graeme Obree's record had been overtaken. The Briton had ridden 52.713km in April 1994. Indurain had ridden 53.040 km, 327 metres further, in spite of having virtually no experience on the track. To succeed though, it was undeniable that Miguel had suffered. Rarely has one seen the Spaniard reach the point where for all he was being followed by the cameras, it was necessary to hold him up as he started to descend the stairs of the velodrome.

Rhythm

The Spaniard had taken a long time to find the right rhythm as he circled the Bordeaux velodrome, before he finally accelerated steadily and irresistably. Obviously his choice of gear - 59x14 - had been the right one. Slower than Obree's time for the first three kilometres (six seconds behind to be exact), from then on he had started to go into the acceleration phase, catching up on Obree by around half a second each lap. "Miguel has started too fast, I'm going to ask him to ease up a bit" decided Doctor Padilla at this point. Indurain had quickly followed his instructions: "It's true, I had started too strongly" he confirmed after his exploit "stronger anyway than I had done in the last training session. And I had faithfully promised that I would stick to the plan we had drawn up of the speeds I was going to reach on each lap."

Sensational

This recovery phase had somewhat slowed his return on Obree's time between the 11th and the 15th kilometre. But Indurain kept his rhythm going perfectly, so effectively indeed that by the end of the 20th kilometre he was in line with the Scot's times again. From that point onwards he was set to improve them by around half a second a kilometre. After 25 kilometres, Miguel hit his definitive cruising speed: one second faster than Obree each kilometre, with a maximum of two seconds reached in the 34th kilometre. The pistons were definitely going full blast then. "Around the 30th kilometre, however, I had a difficult moment. It was in fact the only one in the

whole of my attempt" he commented. "I suffered a lot because of my position on the bike. In a time-trial on the road, you can change your posture a bit and shift around from time to time. Here you had to overcome the pain with changing position come what may. I had to fight myself simply to stay in the same rhythm." After 43 kilometres, Indurain was a whole lap ahead of Obree. "Once in a while I would have a quick glance at the big screen comparing our times. I stuck to the times we had agreed on, but all the way through the attempt I rode in tune with my sensations. I had no pulseometer and so I altered my speed depending on what my body was telling me to do. It was the best way. And I

took exactly the same attitude towards my gear ratio, my bike, my specialised wheels and my triathlete's handlebars."

The wall

The only question left to be answered at that point was if Indurain would be able to break through the wall of 53 kilometres in an hour. He finally rode 53.040. "Personally, my one and only objective was to improve the Hour Record. So much the better if I was able to pass over the obstacle of 53 kilometres. Had I not been able to, it wouldn't have bothered me. My morale was strong. I wanted to succeed but it was terribly

53.040 kilometres in one hour:
Obree's record now belonged to the past.
(Photo: Sergio Penazzo)

draining. Going round a circuit for an hour at maximum speed means appalling pain in the back, the neck, the shoulders and your legs. I don't know if I can go any further. Perhaps there could be another attack on the record next year in Mexico." commented *El Rey*, completely exhausted but also pleased to have overcome an irritating incident. Some weeks before his attack on the Hour Record, Miguel had been suspected of doping in the Tour de L'Oise where traces of salbutamol had been detected in his urine. A substance which he was taking under prescription and for exclusively medical reasons. Furthermore, Miguel had already informed the doctors running the dope control in the Tour de L'Oise that he was taking this substance, and he came out of the affair without any stain on his name.

Bogota

One year later, Miguel Indurain was indeed back on the track fighting for the Hour Record once more. Not in Mexico, but in Bogota, where he had just become World Time-Trial Champion. In Colombia, it was not his own record that he planned to attack, but Tony Rominger's. The Swiss rider had set up a new record some months later in Bordeaux (55.291kms). The Bogota ring was at an altitude of 2,500 metres, which allowed for a considerable degree of rarification in the air. Five kilometres after he started Indurain had a tiny advantage over the Swiss rider: 5-29.18 against 5-30.25. But five kilometres later the trend had changed, Miguel was timed at 11-01 over the same distance which Rominger had covered in 10-53. After 20 kilometres, Indurain was 26 seconds down on the times which his rival had recorded. It was too much, and Miguel put an end to his adventure. And this time it was for good.

World champion and Olympic **champion**

Next to King Juan Carlos with Olano.   (Photo: ESA)

Eddy Merckx has never been overly enthusiastic when talking about Miguel Indurain. Of course the great Eddy has a great deal of respect for the Spaniard's potential as a Tour-man, but he frequently criticises him for his tendency to limit his interests to stage races and, furthermore, avoid the one-day Classics. Undeniably, Indurain has never shone in this area, although exception should be made of his victory in the San Sebastian Classic. What is more, Merckx refused to change his opinion after the World and Olympic time-trial titles which Miguel added to his palmares in Colombia and Atlanta. "I don't understand him" said Eddy one day with complete sincerity "An athlete like Indurain should be able to fight on all fronts. If everybody behaved in the same way, then the majority of riders would refuse to race in the Classics. Miguel is the only one to blame if his palmares does not contain one win in Liège-Bastogne-Liège. He could win

La Doyenne when he felt like it. All he needs is the desire to win it."

Rain

The Spaniard has never agreed at all with Merckxs criticisms. "Each to his own" was his general line of thinking. "In theory, of course, it's true that I could have succeeded in doing great things in one of the Ardennes Classics. In 1991, furthermore, I managed to finish fourth in Liège. But the weather conditions were always too variable. While the sun shone, I felt fine and there was no problem. But the moment the rain or the cold appeared, I lost half my strength. That was one of my worries throughout my entire career: an annoying tendency to catch colds which affected me from then on right up to the last day of racing. That explains why in some years I preferred to ride Tirreno-Adriatico rather than Paris-Nice, and why I preferred the Giro to the Vuelta: in the latter, it was not unheard of for there to be snowstorms at some points. I've spent more than one early season trying to get over a cold or 'flu at home rather than starting my spring preparation in the peloton".

Pavé

If there was one reason why Miguel Indurain failed to turn up at races like the Tour of Flanders or Paris-Roubaix, then it was simply because of the *pavé* which was the main ingredient of such events. It was just the type of terrain he loathed.

"In theory, I had the perfect build to ride over the *pavés* with the best of them. But, not to put too fine a point on it, I did not like them. Just as I absolutely hated the twisty bits which always came before the Flanders hills. I imagine all the riders who specialise in big Tours feel the same kind of aversion towards this sort of course. Ask Pantani what he thinks about it. Furthermore, I hated crashes. I broke my wrist twice in my career, and then I broke my collarbone once as well. Each time it happened was because I was going through a badly surfaced area of the course."

Rainbows

So it can safely be said that Miguel's palmares in one-day races is rather lean. Much leaner than his collection of victories in championships: second and third in the World Road Championships, World Time-Trial Champion in Colombia and Olympic champion in the same speciality in the Atlanta Games. His world title in Colombia was greeted with an exceptional degree of enthusiasm in Spain. This was because at first the reason Miguel had travelled to South America was to try to win the road championships. But the circumstances during the race forced Miguel to work for Olano on that day. In any case Indurain had already won his rainbow jersey in the race against the clock. In that event it took just five kilometres for it to become clear that Indurain was virtually guaranteed to take over from Chris Boardman. At this point in the championship, Indurain was already 18 seconds up on Olano. And after 21 kilometres his advantage had risen to 43. When he crossed the line, the Spaniard was plunged into a genuine hell: the Colombian reporters fought to try and get the best position. Swallowed up in the chaos, unable to breathe in the humid Colombian atmosphere, Indurain took refuge in a little side-road to try and recover.

World Time-Trial Champion.
(Photo: Sergio Penazzo)

On the podium he was positively beaming with delight. "Everybody dreams of becoming world champion one day. In my house it was a kid's dream too" commented a jubilant Miguel. "I started very fast to try and establish a large gap. Half way down the route, I overtook Fondriest. I thought that was the best moment to ease up a little. And from that moment onwards, I changed my tempo depending on what my main rival, Olano, did."

Miguel finally won his World gold medal.
(Photo: Sergio Penazzo)

Gold

But his victory at Atlanta was doubtless a far more important occasion. However, in terms of morale, one could have thought that Indurain would not be at his best after his defeat in the Tour. But Indurain continued training in preparation for the Olympic Games. Of course, this Olympic time-trial title was never going to compensate totally for his defeat in the *Grand Boucle*, but the look of sheer delight on the face of the Navarran rider when he took the gold medal was there for all to see, and he raised his arms to the sky as a sign of his pleasure at winning. It was a gesture which clearly expressed his intense joy - because Indurain, it should be remembered, was generally far more given to hiding his emotions behind a screen of coldness.

An Olympic gold. (Photo: AP)

Juan Carlos

The Olympic time-trial race was a highly charged event, if a little distorted by the varying weather conditions. Some riders were forced to take to the course in the rain, while others rolled down the start ramp to find themselves racing on dry terrain. Boardman had had the best start. But the Briton rapidly began to crack, making mistakes as to which route to choose in exactly the same spots where Indurain took the route with perfect mastery. The Spaniard decided to use a conventional road bike, equipped with normal wheels. He tackled the course at an average speed of 48.87 kph. By kilometre 39 he was already 12 seconds ahead of Boardman, while Olano had been timed 20 seconds behind the Briton. Olano pulled back eight seconds in his favour thanks to a fantastic last lap of the circuit, a recovery which finally enabled him to drop Boardman. But against *The Master* in person, even the powerful Abraham was unable to do anything: he finished 13 seconds behind Indurain in the final results. "This gold medal takes on a really special importance in my eyes" commented Miguel. "A lot of people are apparently going to try to question its value. But for me, this is a truly historic moment in my career."
However, some time later, Indurain refused to accept the invitation made by King Juan Carlos, who granted all the Spanish medal-winners from this Olympic Games an audience.

The future:
a time for reflection

Miguel Indurain is a kind, pleasant, straightforward sort of chap, always polite and discreet. The Spaniard has never been and doubtless never will be a good communicator, even in the new life which he has just begun. In his earliest days Miguel had to learn his father's profession. But from the moment his own son was born that was his new reason to live, and his wife Marisa loves nothing more than long family conversations around the coffee table. Even when he had formed part of the peloton, Miguel had already bought a second home in Benidorm. He frequently takes his young family there, especially now he no longer has to face up to strict professional obligations. Apparently, the last thing that Indurain is after is a new profession. This is doubtless what caused the final connection to be broken between himself

and Banesto, his former sponsor. He could have had a job there as a P.R. man for the rest of his days, but he turned down the offer. Miguel had no further contact with his *directeur sportif*, José Miguel Echavarri. During the Vuelta in 1996, the relationship between the former champion and the person who had been his one time confidente, his protector and his right-hand man had irreversibly broken down. In any case Indurain had refused to let his new situation force him into a major depression. "Riders of that kind of calibre don't really ever suffer so badly when they stop racing" considers Eddy Merckx. "Quite the opposite in fact, they really enjoy the sudden sensation of calm. At first the top priority on retiring is to enjoy a sense of relaxation and undisturbed well-being. But when the time arrives to start thinking about another

Well-mannered, charming and rather quiet.
(Photo: Graham Watson)

activity they generally have no lack of choice. The offers come pouring in. The only really important thing is that they do something they enjoy and that they're interested in."

Mr PR man.   (Photo: Rudi Van Beek)

Ten kilos

The newly-retired rider was visibly content with his lot. In fact he did not change too deeply in a physical sense. Looking ultra-smart in a black suit which showed off his smart haircut, he could easily have found a job as a male model - using his appearance and good looks. In slightly less than two years, Indurain has put on only ten kilos. "The form has long since been forgotten, it is just a vague memory at most. I have started taking the bike out again; two or three times a week at most, for around 60 kilometres. But my legs have got really heavy now. When there's a

headwind or the road starts to climb, I turn round and head for home again in two shakes of a lamb's tail! Occasionally I go with my brother Prudencio on his training rides, but I don't look after him in his career in general. He is more than experienced enough to know what he's doing. It's certainly not up to me to tell him what to do."

Ghost town

Miguel Indurain is not the type of person who beats around the bush. For him black is black and white is white. And he has certainly never felt the need to be coy about his feelings. "I am in a period of transition" explains the five-time winner of the Tour de France as if he wanted to justify his period of inactivity. "We will see, later, what is the right direction to take. I've been told that I have bought a whole town somewhere in Spain, and also that I have dreams of starting up a huge agricultural enterprise. I have even heard that I've started working in construction. That apart, the fact that I have in fact invested something - together with Marino Lejaretta - in a supermarket selling sports products doesn't really indicate what road I will finally take. I'm taking my time to work out what my possible options are. For the moment, I spend some of my time as a P.R. man. You could say that this involves hiring myself out to these companies, and I represent their products."

Suitcases

There is a world of difference between Indurain and the other big cyclists. After his career, the Spaniard has preferred to seek out a refuge in his family, breaking completely with all the razzmatazz of the professional circuit. This is the complete opposite of Bernard Hinault, for example, who has never really been able to tear

With his wife Marisa and their son Miguel junior. (Photo: Jan Van der Perre)

himself away himself from the *milieu*, or Eddy Merckx, whose heart beats in time to the current developments in the world of cycling. Miguel, on the other hand, has put a gap between himself and that world. In the World Championships at San Sebastian, for example, he just came along as a simple member of the public, nothing more. "That's true, ever since I hung up my wheels, I have never had the slightest shred of nostalgia. I am still a huge fan of cycling as a sport, but in the same way that any normal spectator would be. I have never thought of becoming a *directeur sportif*, for example. That is out of the question. And my contacts with my former "work-mates" are simply chance meetings. I only go very occasionally to races. What would I do there, I ask you? Doubtless within a few years I will change my point of view. But for now, I have no feeling that I really need to return to that kind of atmosphere. I did meet Abraham Olano one day: it was by chance on the tarmac of an airport. We were both carryinng our suitcases to get different planes."

Nature

Miguel Indurain no longer has to work to earn his living. The Navarran giant is immensely rich. At the peak of his career, bearing in mind the innumerable publicity contracts which went naturally with his star status, he earned around 90 million francs (nine million pounds sterling). Now he can profit from that huge fortune constructed by his legs. "I don't want to face up to the slightest obligation. I just want to do what I want to do. Like, for example, travelling all over the place. Recently we went on holiday to Switzerland. It was a wonderful rest, where I really felt in contact with nature. I love wandering around the mountains, going out and seeing animals. I've also been with Marisa to Germany on a number of occasions. For now, I simply enjoy my sense of calm. In the winter, I hunt. I lived like a monk for a long time and that period of my life is well and truly over. As a rider, I was lucky enough to go through some really beautiful areas. I have written them all down in a notebook and from now on it's information for the benefit of my wife."

In the race director's car during the Tour.
(Photo: AP)

Nothing for free

Miguel Indurain married Marisa Lopez de Goicoechea, a very smart young lady with dark hair. "I met her in a hospital in Pamplona. She worked there as a nurse and I used to go in regularly for check-ups. What happened afterwards is easy to imagine" remembers Miguel, clearly completely enthralled by his family. "I am and always will remain a man of the soil. My parents, as smallholders, have managed to transmit me that love of work. Cycle racing has one thing in common with work in the field, that you have to work your finger to the bone just to get the slightest reward. Nature doesn't give anything away to those she feeds. And the same goes for sport. I am happy about the education I have received from my parents. I didn't become a champion just like that, I was born one. But I had to invest an enormous amount of time and effort to make that innate

talent bear fruit. That's the reason why, now, I have no desire at all to sweat. My parents did not decide on my future in cycling. They simply wanted what was best for me. At first the bike was simply a practical means of transport for getting about the country. When I used to come back home from school and I found out which part of the farm my father was working on, I would jump on the bike to go and join him and lend him a hand. He was disappointed when I decided to stop studying to start racing. In our home, the bike was simply a way of getting from a to b, a tool pure and simple. Lots of people think that this kind of necessity is a part of the making of the great champions. I don't agree. And what's more, I am convinced that I could have found my way in life without ever having ridden a bike."

Miguel Indurain Larraya
Palmares

1983 Amateur
Navarran championships; Spanish national championships.

1984 Reynolds
2 wins: Tour de L'Avenir, stage 3 and time trial.

1985 Reynolds
2 wins: Tour de L'Avenir, stage 6 and stage 11 (time trial).
Other important results: Ruta del Sol (2nd); Tour of Spain (84th); Spanish national championships (52nd).

1986 Reynolds
6 wins: Tour of Murcia, prologue and final overall; Tour de L'Avenir: prologue, stage nine and final overall; Leiza.
Other important results: Ruta del Sol (5th); Tour of Spain (92nd); Midi Libre (6th); Spanish national championships (6th); Zizurkil (3rd); GP des Nations (14th).

1987 Reynolds
12 wins: Tour of Murcia, prologue; Catalan Week, stages 3, 5 and 6; Tour of the Mining Valleys, stages 3, 4 and final overall; Tour of Galicia, stage 1; Memorial Saint André; stage and final overall Salita Txitxarro.
Other important results: Ponferrada (5th); Spanish national championships (4th); Tour de France (97th); Bilbao (2nd); Tour of Galicia (8th); World Championships (64th); Tour of La Rioja (5th).

1988 Reynolds
4 wins: Tour of Cantabria, stage 4; Tour of Galicia, stage 2; Tour of Catalonia, stage 6 and final overall.
Other important results: Ruta del Sol (13th); Catalan Week (8th); Spanish national championships (55th); Tour de France (47th); Tour of Burgos (12th); San Sebastian Classic (6th); Tour of Galicia (3rd); Joué-les-Tours (2nd); Navarre (4th).

1989 Reynolds
8 wins: Paris-Nice; 2nd stage and final overall Criterium International; Tour de France stage 9; Manlleu omnium; Tarragona omnium (with Melchior Mauri); Pamplona omnium; Alquerias omnium.
Other important results: Tour of Valencia (5th); Milan-San Remo (42nd); Navarre (5th); Flèche Wallone (7th); Liège-Bastogne-Liège (10th); Tour of Switzerland (10th); Spanish national championships (39th); Tour de France (17th); G.P. Americas (30th); San Sebastian Classic (36th); Tour of Galicia (7th); Marostica (3rd); Tour of Catalonia (10th); Subida a Naranco (2nd).

1990 Banesto
8 wins: Tour of Valencia, stage 5; Paris-Nice, stage 6 and final overall; Tour of the Basque Country, stage 5; Tour de France, stage 16; Tarnos criterium; Tour of Burgos stage 6; San Sebastian Classic.
Other important results: GP Luis Puig (5th); Tour of Valencia (9th); Criterium International (7th); Bicicleta Vasca (3rd); Flèche Wallone (4th); Liège-Bastogne-Liège (12th); Amstel Gold (19th); Tour of Spain (7th); Tour of Asturias (3rd), Bicicleta Eibarresa (4th); Spanish national championship (3rd); Tour de France (10th); Tour of Burgos (3rd); Subida a Urkiola (7th); Zurich Championship (39th); World Championships - Utsunomiya (12th).

1991 Banesto
15 wins: Tour de Vaucluse, stage 2 and final overall; Navarre; Tour of the Basque Country stages 2 and 5; Tour de France, stages 8, 21 and final overall; Castillon-la-Bataille; Tour of Catalonia, stage 5 and final overall; Toulouse criterium; Alqerias criterium; Fuenlabrada criterium; Alcobendas omnium.
Other important results: Milan-San Remo (124th); Flèche Wallone (17th); Liège-Bastogne-Liège (4th); Tour of Spain (2nd); Tour of Asturias (6th); Bicicleta Vasca (3rd); Spanish national championships (82nd); San Sebastian Classic (14th); Zurich Championship (100th); World Championships - Stuttgart (3rd).

1992 Banesto
18 wins: Tour of Romandie, stage 4; Tour of Italy, stages 4, 22 and overall; Spanish national championship; Tour de France, prologue, stages 9, 19 and final overall; Monein; Castilla-Leon Trophy, stage 1; Chateaulin; Tour of Catalonia, final overall; Oviedo omnium; Fuenlabrada omnium; Rafaelbunyo omnium; Hernani omnium; Alquerias criterium.
Other important results: Tour of Valencia (24th); Paris-Nice (3rd), Milan-San Remo (167th); Tour of Aragon (4th); Tour of Romandy (2nd); Tour de L'Oise (3rd); Chateau-Chinon 2nd); Emmen (3rd); Castilla-Leon Trophy (15th); World Championships - Benidorm, 6th; Subida a Naranco (5th); Alcobendas (2nd); Alquerias (2nd).

1993 Banesto

Velo D'Or

18 wins: Tour of Murcia, stage 6; Tour of Italy, stages 10, 19, and final overall; Tour of the Mining Valleys, stages 2 and 4; Tour de France, prologue, time-trial and final overall; Castille-Leon Trophy, prologue and final overall; Tour of the Puertos; Valladolid omnium; Oviedo omnium; Salamanca omnium; Alquerias omnium; Rafaelbunyol omnium; Alcobendas omnium.

Other important results: Almeria (7th); Milan-San Remo (123rd); Liège-Bastogne-Liège (51st); Amstel Gold (72nd); Gippingen (8th); Tour of Romandie (15th); Tour of the Mining Valleys (13th); Spanish national championships (2nd); World Championships - Oslo (2nd); Tour of Catalonia (4th); Saragossa (4th).

1994 Banesto

World Hour Record in Bordeaux: 53.040 kms

12 wins: Tour of Valencia, stage 6; Tour de L'Oise, stage 4 and final overall; Tour de France, stage 9 and final overall; Castille-la-Bataille; Castille-Leon Trophy, stage 3; Valladolid omnium; Salamanca omnium; Fuenlabrada omnium; Durango omnium; Gran Canaria omnium.

Other important results: Tour of Valencia (2nd); Paris-Nice (35th); Milan-San Remo (31st); Tour of Romandie (35th); Tour of Italy (3rd); San Sebastian Classic (41st); Alquerias (2nd); Gandia (4th); Alcobendas (2nd); Saragossa (3rd); Segovia (3rd); Lanzarote (3rd); Tenerife (2nd).

1995 Banesto

18 wins: Tour of Aragon, stage 4; Tour of the Mining Valleys, stage 4; Tour of La Rioja, stage 1 sectors A and B, and final overall; Tour of Asturias, stage 1 and final overall; Midi Libre, final overall; Dauphiné Libéré, stage 3 and final overall; Tour de France, stages 8, 19 and final overall; Moscow; Tour of Galicia, stage 1 and final overall; Rominger Classic Crans Montana; World Championships - Tunja (time-trial).

Other important results: Milan-San Remo (132nd); Tour of Aragon (4th); Amstel Gold Race (31st); Tour of the Mining Valleys (3rd); Classique des Alpes (6th); Spanish national championships (6th); San Sebastian Classic (9th); Colorado Classic (2nd); World Road Championships - Duitama (2nd).

1996 Banesto

18 wins: Tour of Alentejo, stages 1, 5 and final overall; Tour of Asturias, stage 1 and final overall; Bicicleta Vasca, stage 5 and final overall; Dauphiné Libéré, 2 stages and final overall; Olympic time-trial - Atlanta; Colmar criterium; Llobregat criterium; Pamplona omnium; Fuenblabrada omnium; Malaga omnium; Xativa omnium.

Other important results: Milan-San Remo (115th); Tour of Aragon (4th); Amstel Gold (26th); Classique des Alpes (8th); Spanish national championships (37th); Tour de France (11th); Olympic road championships (26th); San Sebastian Classic (12th); Tour of Burgos (2nd); G.P. Suisse (41st); Tour of Venice (24th).

This book, 'Indurain', is the first in the CycleScoop series, in which Noël Truyers presents a portrait of some major names in the international cycling peloton.
"Indurain" will be followed in 1999 by books on Sean Kelly, Stephen Roche, Jan Raas and Herman Vanspringel.

Acknowledgements

'De Eecloonaar' Publications
Industrielaan 44
9900 - Eeklo - Belgium
Tel: 00 32 (0) 93771182
Fax: 00 32 (0) 93781234
Internet: www.eecloonaar.be

Author: Noël Truyers
Project, layout, setup and printing:
'de Eecloonaar' printers
Industrielaan 44 - 9900 Eeklo

Bookbinders: Proost, Turnhout (B)

Translation: Alasdair Fotheringham

Book available in English, Dutch, French and Spanish

ISBN 90-74128-34-3
Legal number D/1998/5813/18
Copyright 1999 Eecloonaar Publications

Photos and illustrations:

Photos have been placed at our disposition by the RUG archives, Luc Daelemans, the Club Ciclista Villavés, Sergio Penazzo, Rudi Van Beek, Jan Van Der Perre and Graham Watson.
In the event of the publication of photos not being the subject of a demand of authorization, being of unknown origin, the author should get in touch with the editor.